I ♥ BEES

Buster Books

Illustrated by
Lizzie Preston and
Charlotte Pepper

Edited by Emma Taylor
Cover Design by Derrian Bradder
Designed by Jade Moore

First published in Great Britain in 2021 by Buster Books, an imprint of
Michael O'Mara Books Limited, 9 Lion Yard, Tremadoc Road, London SW4 7NQ

W www.mombooks.com/buster **f** Buster Books **🐦** @BusterBooks **📷** @Buster_Books

ISBN: 978-1-78055-764-9

2 4 6 8 10 9 7 5 3 1

This book was printed in April 2021 by
Bell & Bain Limited, 303 Burnfield Road, Thornliebank,
Glasgow, G46 7UQ, United Kingdom.

MIX
Paper from
responsible sources
FSC® C007785
www.fsc.org

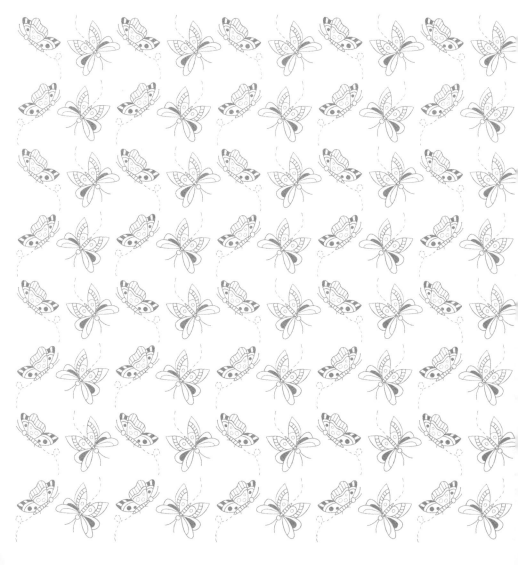

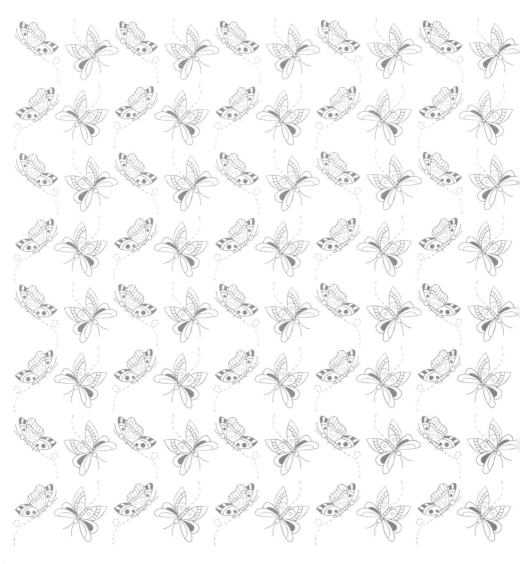

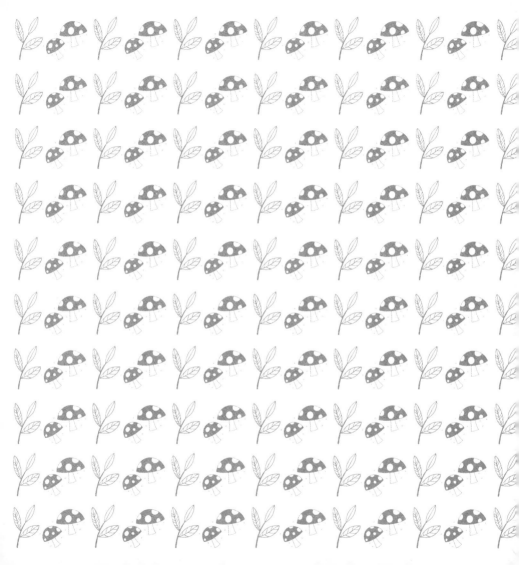

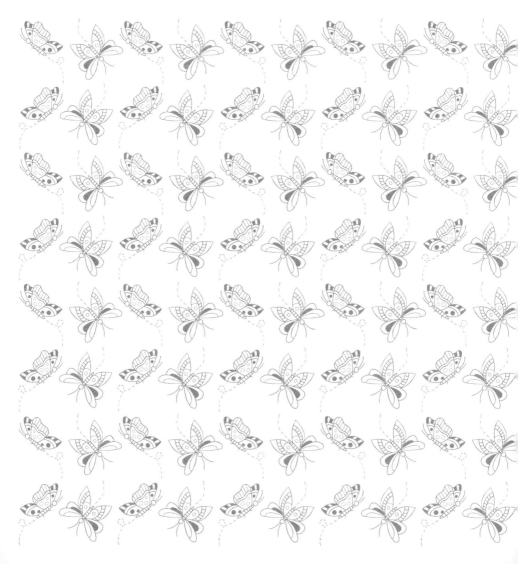

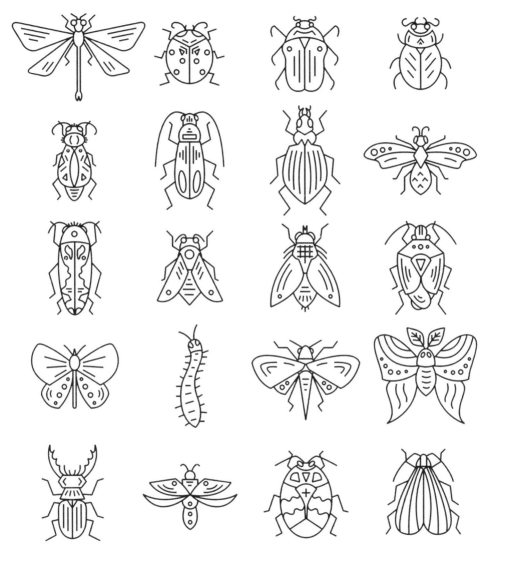

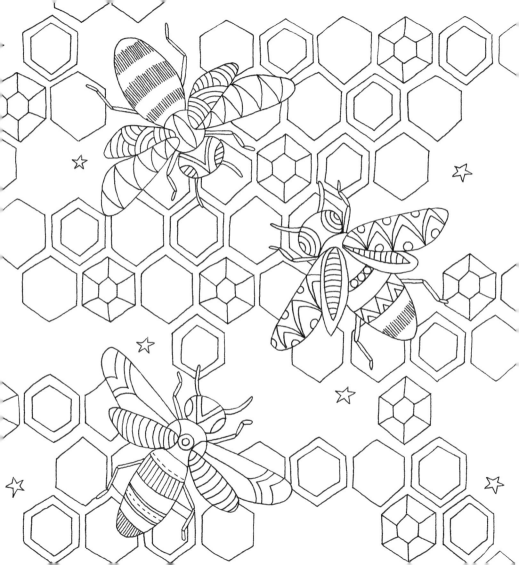

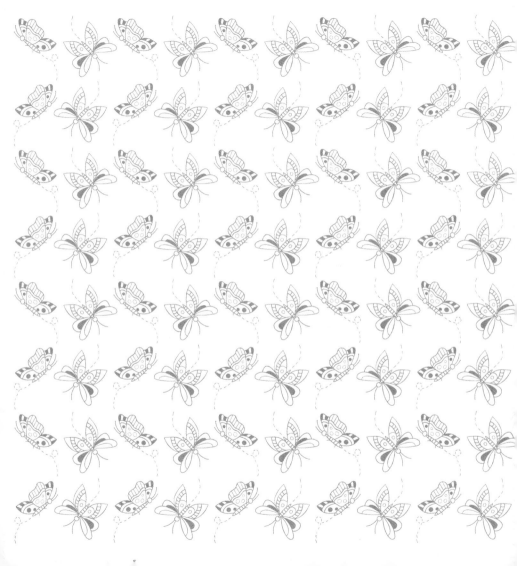

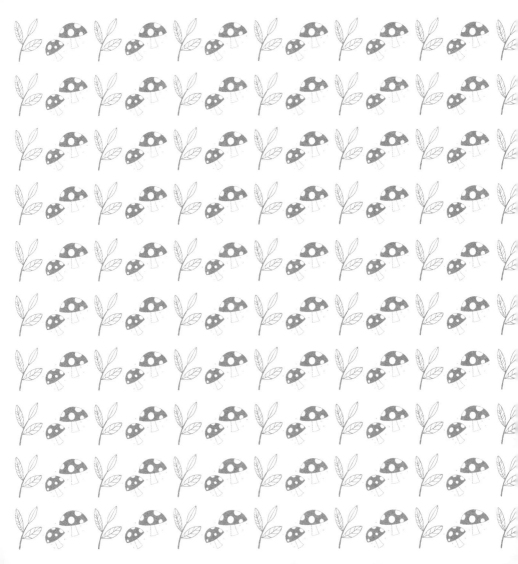

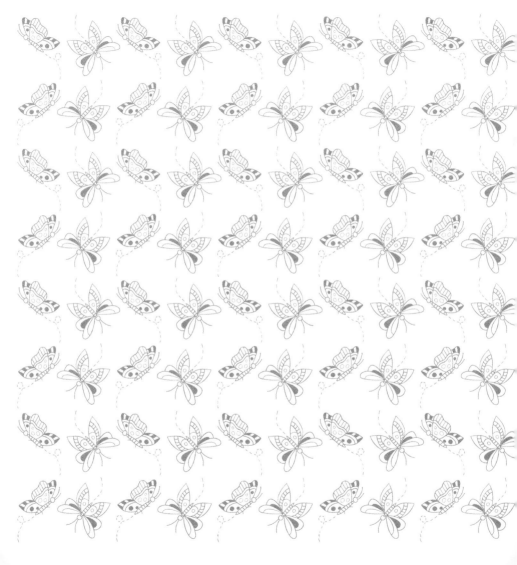

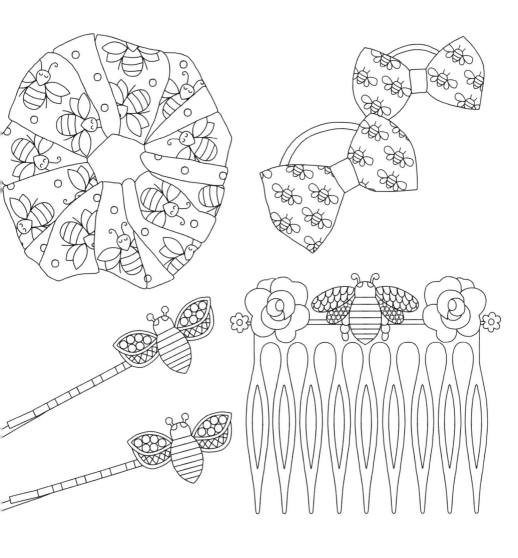

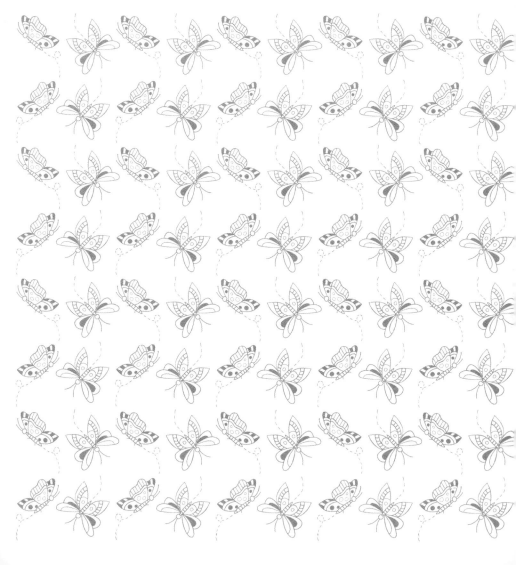

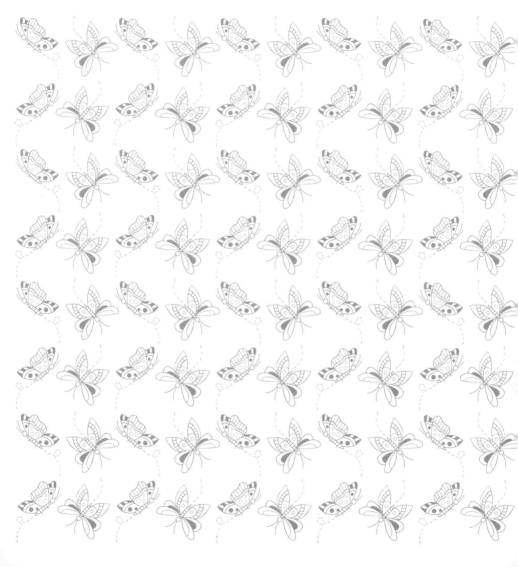

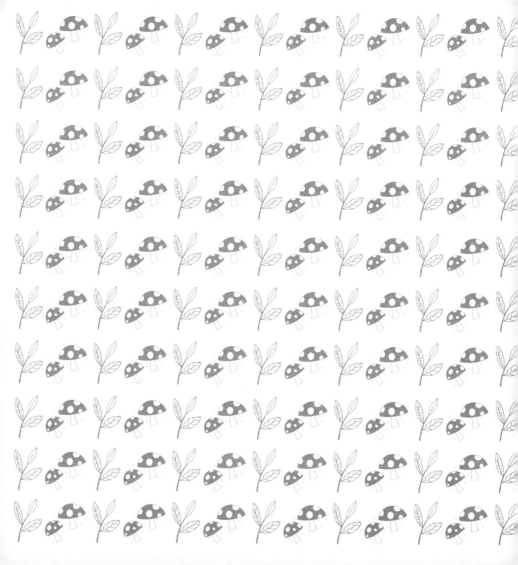

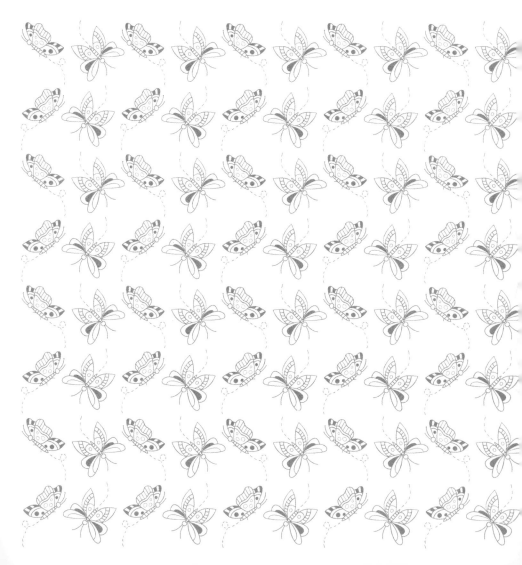

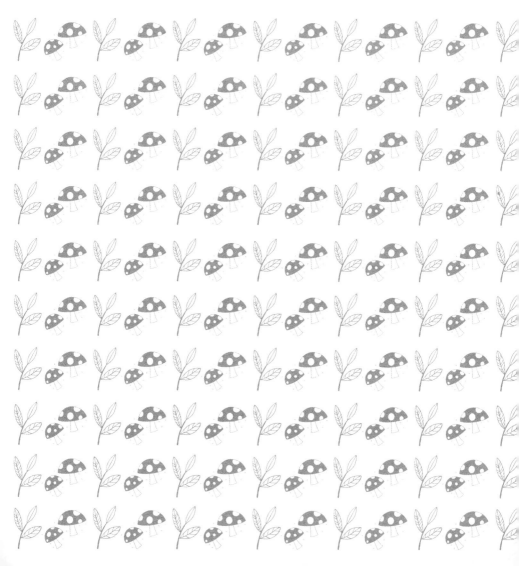

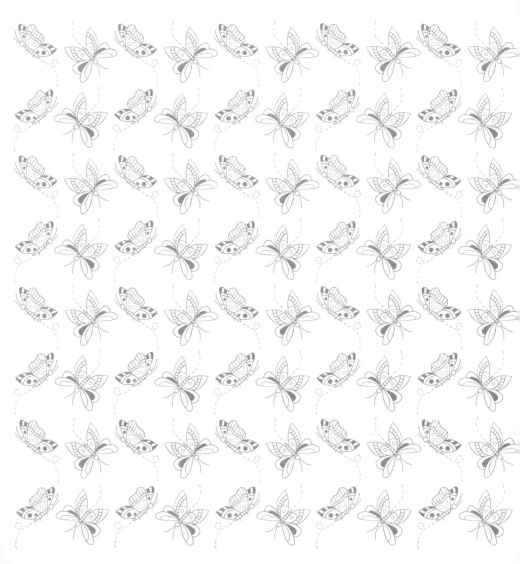

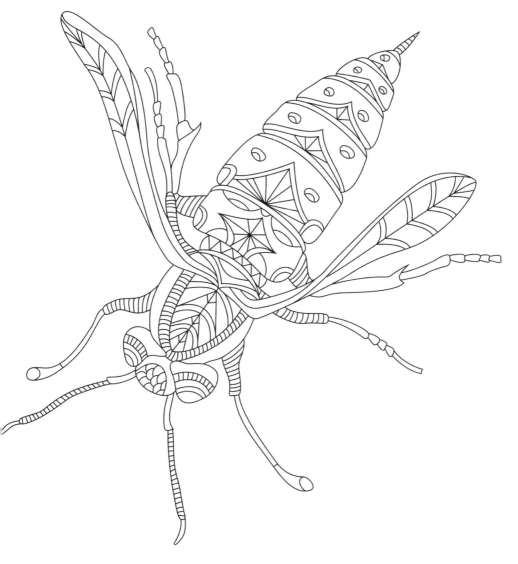

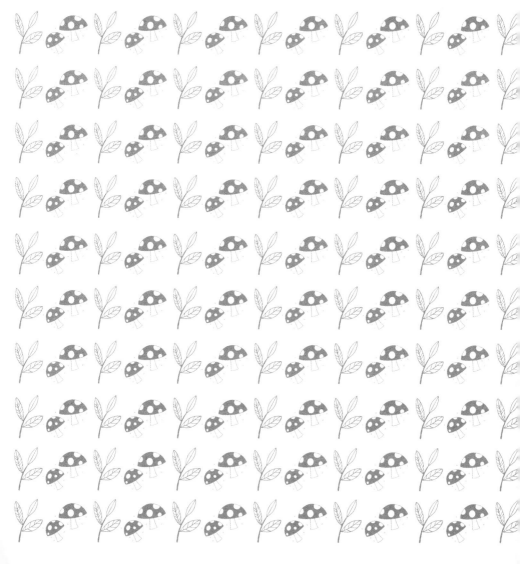

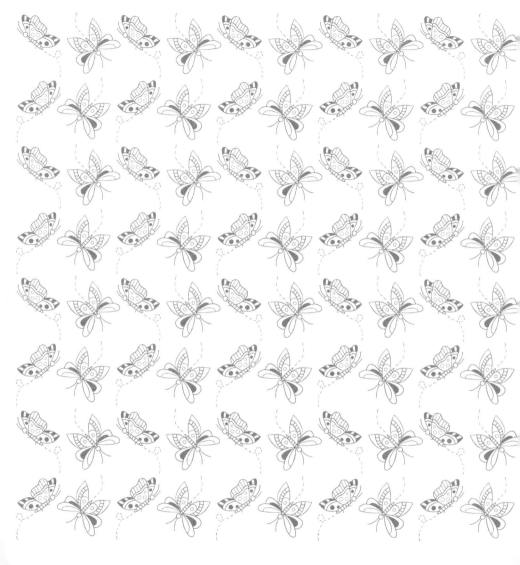

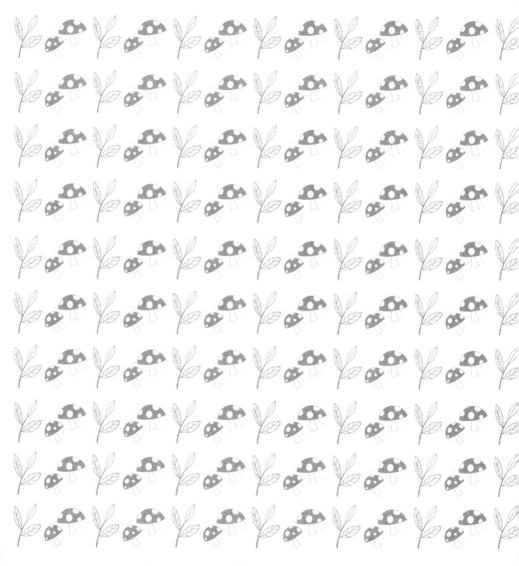

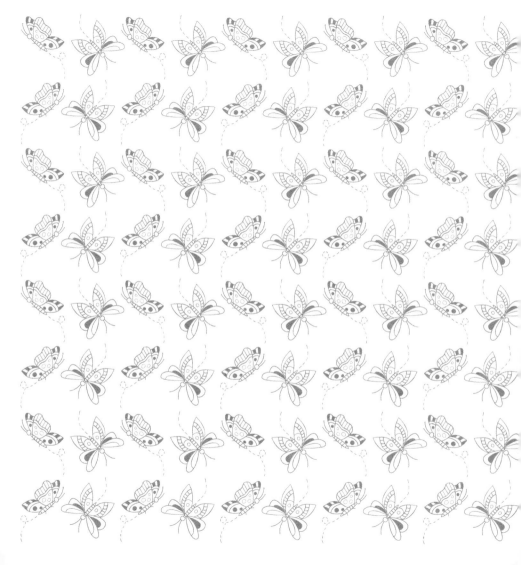

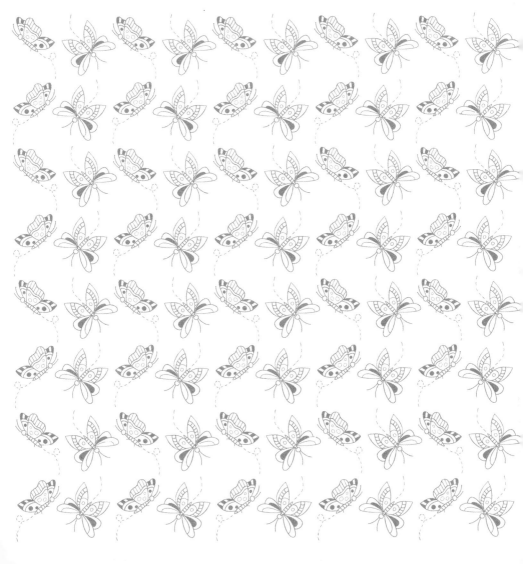

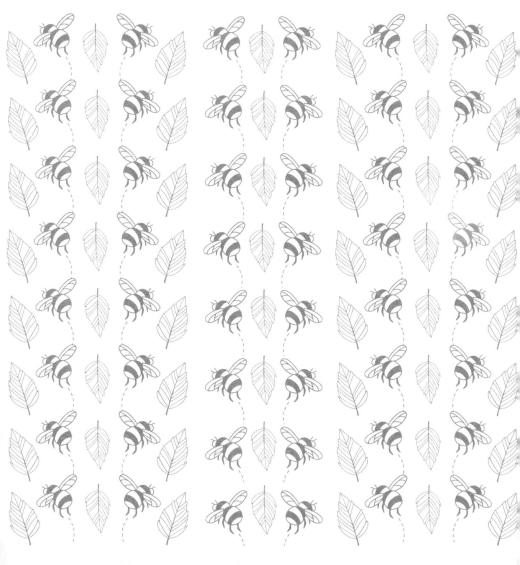